At Sylvan, we believe reading is one of life's most important and enriching abilities, and we're glad you've chosen our resources to help your child build these critically important skills. We know that the time you spend with your child reinforcing the lessons learned in school will contribute to his love of reading. This love of reading will translate into academic achievement. A successful reader is ready for the world around him, ready to do research, ready to experience the world of literature, and prepared to make the connections necessary to achieve in school and in life.

We use a research-based, step-by-step process in teaching reading at Sylvan that includes thought-provoking reading selections and activities. As students increase their success as readers they become more confident. With increasing confidence, students build even more success. Our Sylvan workbooks are designed to help you to help your child build the skills and confidence that will contribute to your child's success in school.

Included with your purchase of this workbook is a coupon for a discount at a participating Sylvan center. We hope you will use this coupon to further your child's academic journey. Let us partner with you to support the development of a confident, well prepared, independent learner.

The Sylvan Team

Sylvan Learning Center.
Unleash your child's potential here.

No matter how big or small the academic challenge, every child has the ability to learn. But sometimes children need help making it happen. Sylvan believes every child has the potential to do great things. And, we know better than anyone else how to tap into that academic potential so that a child's future really is full of possibilities. Sylvan Learning Center is the place where your child can build and master the learning skills needed to succeed and unlock the potential you know is there.

The proven, personalized approach of our in-center programs deliver unparalleled results that other supplemental education services simply can't match. Your child's achievements will be seen not only in test scores and report cards but outside the classroom as well. And when he starts achieving his full potential, everyone will know it. You will see a new level of confidence come through in everything he does and every interaction he has.

How can Sylvan's personalized in-center approach help your child unleash his potential?

• Starting with our exclusive Sylvan Skills Assessment®, we pinpoint your child's exact academic needs.

• Then we develop a customized learning plan designed to achieve your child's academic goals.

• Through our method of skill mastery, your child will not only learn and master every skill in his personalized plan, he will be truly motivated and inspired to achieve his full potential.

To get started, included with this Sylvan product purchase is $10 off our exclusive Sylvan Skills Assessment®. Simply use this coupon and contact your local Sylvan Learning Center to set up your appointment.

And to learn more about Sylvan and our innovative in-center programs, call 1-800-EDUCATE or visit www.SylvanLearning.com. *With over 1,000 locations in North America, there is a Sylvan Learning Center near you!*

2nd Grade Spelling
Games & Activities

Published in the United States by Random House, Inc., New York, and in Canada by Random House of Canada Limited, Toronto.

www.tutoring.sylvanlearning.com

Created by Smarterville Productions LLC
Producer: TJ Trochlil McGreevy
Producer & Editorial Direction: The Linguistic Edge
Writer: Michael Artin
Cover and Interior Illustrations: Duendes del Sur
Layout and Art Direction: SunDried Penguin
Art Manager: Adina Ficano

First Edition

ISBN: 978-0-375-43028-2

Library of Congress Cataloging-in-Publication Data available upon request.

This book is available at special discounts for bulk purchases for sales promotions or premiums. For more information, write to Special Markets/Premium Sales, 1745 Broadway, MD 6-2, New York, New York 10019 or e-mail specialmarkets@randomhouse.com.

PRINTED IN CHINA

10 9 8 7 6 5 4 3 2 1

Contents

Spell Short Vowels

Puzzle Pairs

FILL IN the two different missing vowels in the word pairs to finish the riddles.

1. This beetle was not small.

   He was a **b__g b__g.**

2. When I left my cap on the stove, I had a **h__t h__t.**

3. I did not sleep well last night. I was on a **b__d b__d.**

4. To get pecans out of the tree,

   I used a **n__t n__t.**

5. The rabbit went **h__p h__p** all

   the way up the hill.

Criss Cross

READ the clues. FILL IN the boxes with the right word for each clue.

Across

1. This says "meow."
3. You clean the floor with this.
6. My cat or my dog is my ____.
8. A hole in the ground
10. "You are it!" in the game of ____
11. You sleep here.

Down

2. The highest spot
4. A young dog
5. You ____ a ball with a bat.
7. Wash up in the bath____.
9. One after nine.

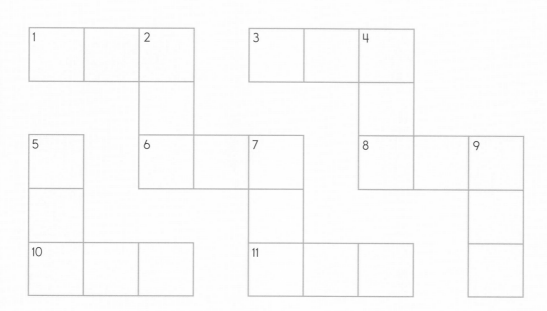

Puzzle Pairs

FILL IN the missing vowels in the word pairs to finish the sentences. Listen for how the final "-e" changes the vowel sound.

1. When it's my turn,

   I **h__p__** I can **h__p**.

2. My sister broke my toy. It **m__d__** me **m__d**.

3. Pete is my dog. If you want, you can **p__t** **P__t__**.

4. Maya went to the salon and got a **c__t__** **c__t**.

5. The shark was a star.

   He had a **f__n__** **f__n**.

Not Quite!

CIRCLE the words that are misspelled in this story.

I saw a very cut kitten. I gav him a pok. That mad him hid from me. I hat when that happens! I hop I see him again some tim.

WRITE the circled words correctly.

1. _____

2. _____

3. _____

4. _____

5. _____

6. _____

7. _____

8. _____

Blank Out

FILL IN the missing "ch," "sh," "wh," or "th" in these sentences.

SPELLING LIST

chat
chick
chop
shapes
ship
shop
shut
thick
thin
what
when
white

1. Miguel was _____**ite** as a ghost!

2. I always cry when I _____**op** onions.

3. Yay! Mom gave me a _____**ick** slice of cake!

4. Tom helps his dad _____**op** for food.

5. I want to hear about your day.

   Let's have a little _____**at**.

6. Bella went for a cruise on a _____**ip**.

7. Grandma always feeds me too much.

   She says I look _____**in**.

8. Close the washer door _____**en**

   you wash your clothes.

Match Up

DRAW a line to the correct word ending.

1. **ch**

en   ick

2. **wh**

ite   ig

3. **sh**

apes   ogs

4. **sh**

ig   ip

5. **ch**

an   op

6. **sh**

op   ug

Word Scramble

UNSCRAMBLE each word and write it correctly. LOOK at the word box for help.
CROSS OUT each word as you make it.

| thin | thick | chop | chick | chat | shop | ship | shapes | what | white |

1. hpis _____

2. tnih _____

3. ahtw _____

4. kichc _____

5. ithew _____

6. ohpc _____

7. thac _____

8. spesah _____

9. citkh _____

10. psoh _____

Riddle Me This!

UNSCRAMBLE the words in the riddles.

1. **Q.** Why did the bookworm start eating the

   dictionary at T?

   A. He wanted to eat through **chitk** and **inht**.

   _____ _____

2. **Q.** What do you call talking while eggs hatch?

   A. A **ccikh thca**.

   _____ _____

3. **Q.** Why did the captain build his house like a boat?

   A. He liked things **isph aphes**.

   _____

   _____

Ending Consonant Combos

Blank Out!

FILL IN the missing "th," "sh," "ch," or "tch" in these sentences.

SPELLING LIST

bath
math
with
dash
fish
rich
which
catch
watch
witch

1. Johnny ate **fi**_____ sticks for lunch.

2. Come **wi**_____ me to the fair.

3. Tim wondered **whi**_____ way to go.

4. My **wa**_____ says it's five-thirty.

5. Julie was the winner of the 100-yard **da**_____.

6. I like numbers, so **ma**_____ is fun for me.

7. Becky put on her **wi**_____ costume for the party.

8. Kim didn't think she'd **ca**_____ such a big fish!

Word Split

DRAW lines to connect word beginnings with the correct endings.

1.
 **ba**

 **ch**

2.
 **ri**

 **sh**

3.
 **ca**

 **th**

4.
 **da**

 **tch**

Ending Consonant Combos

Word Blocks

FILL IN the word blocks with words of the same shape from the word box. Use the pictures as clues.

rich   fish   bath   math   witch   watch

2+3=5

1.

2.

3.

4.

5.

6.

Not Quite!

CIRCLE the words that are misspelled in this story.

Sam caught a fish, whish made him happy.

"I am really a wich," it said. "Throw me back, and I will make you ritsh."

"But I might not catsh another fish," said Sam.

"You can buy another one," said the fich. "Come on! Do the maf!"

Sam ate him wif a datsh of salt.

WRITE the circled words correctly.

1. _____   5. _____

2. _____   6. _____

3. _____   7. _____

4. _____   8. _____

Word Scramble

UNSCRAMBLE each word and write it correctly. LOOK at the word box for help.
CROSS OUT each word in the word box as you make it.

belt   coat   dress   pants   shirt   shorts   skirt   shoe

SPELLING LIST

belt
coat
dress
pants
shirt
shoe
shorts
skirt

1. sreds _____

2. tisrk _____

3. strih _____

4. atoc _____

5. hoes _____

6. elbt _____

7. rhtoss _____

8. snapt _____

Word Hunt

CIRCLE the words from the word box in the grid. Words go down and across, not diagonally or backward.

belt   coat   dress   pants   shirt   shorts   skirt   shoe

```
b  o  r  t  s  p  o  e
e  r  s  s  e  a  k  r
l  c  o  k  c  n  i  a
t  s  h  i  r  t  r  p
s  h  d  r  e  s  s  n
c  o  a  t  s  h  o  i
o  e  s  h  o  r  t  s
```

WRITE each word that you circled.

_____   _____

_____   _____

_____   _____

_____   _____

Sort and Spell

LISTEN for the **ch** or **sh** sound at the start or end of each word pictured. DRAW a line from the picture to the correct sound box. WRITE the word in the box.

shoe	chick	rich	ship	chop	fish

ch

_____

_____

_____

sh

_____

_____

_____

Around We Go!

CIRCLE the things that have a **ch** sound. Write the words on the lines.

_____ _____

_____

Criss Cross

READ the clues. FILL IN the boxes with the right word for each clue.

Across

3. _____ way did he go?
5. Something that sails on the sea
7. Opposite of fat
8. The rhino has very _____ skin.
10. To cut a tree with an ax
13. The color of milk
14. You throw the ball, and I will _____ it.
15. Working with numbers

Down

1. A square is a _____, and so is a triangle.
2. You wear this to cover your belly
4. In the summer you wear these so your legs stay cool
6. A swimming animal
9. A baby hen
11. You tuck your shirt into your _____.
12. This helps hold up your pants
14. Two people talking are having a _____.

Beginning Consonant Blends

Knock Out

CROSS OUT the pictures whose words **don't** begin with two consonant sounds together.

SPELLING LIST

clam
crab
frog
slide
slip
spill
steps
stick
stop
trap
trip
truck

WRITE the words for the pictures you didn't cross out.

_____   _____

_____   _____

Blank Out

FILL IN the missing letters for each word.

 1. __ __ am

 4. __ __ og

 2. __ __ ill

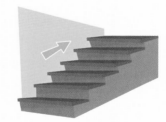 5. __ __ eps

 3. __ __ ap

 6. __ __ ab

Beginning Consonant Blends

Puzzle Pairs

FILL IN the missing letters in the word pairs to finish these sentences.

1. The firefighters **tuck** their shirts in before they get

   on the **t__uck**.

2. The **fog** was so thick at the pond I couldn't even

   see a **f__og** jump.

3. I felt **sick** about breaking grandpa's walking **s__ick**.

4. **Tap** him on the shoulder and warn him. This is

   a **t__ap**.

5. Take a **sip** from the stream, but don't **s__ip** and

   fall in!

6. I took a **cab** to the beach, where I saw a **c__ab**.

7. Chang peeked over the **side** before he went down

   the **s__ide**.

8. Here's a **tip**: Be careful not to **t__ip**.

Word Scramble

UNSCRAMBLE the words. LOOK at the word box for help. CROSS OUT each word in the word box as you make it.

clam	frog	slide	stick	steps	trip
crab	slip	spill	stop	truck	trap

1. ipsl _____

2. rtpa _____

3. pesst _____

4. amlc _____

5. skict _____

6. barc _____

7. ospt _____

8. lispl _____

9. ilsed _____

10. prit _____

11. orgf _____

12. urckt _____

Ending Consonant Blends

Blank Out

FILL IN the missing pair of letters at the end of each word.

SPELLING LIST

gift
lamp
camp
jump
desk
mask
band
hand
ant
tent
cast
nest

 1. ha _ _ _

 4. gi _ _ _

 2. de _ _ _

 5. ne _ _ _

 3. la _ _ _

 6. ma _ _ _

7. ju __ __

10. a __ __

8. te __ __

11. ca __ __

9. ca __ __

12. ba __ __

Not Quite!

CIRCLE the words that are misspelled in this story.

Hank made a capm. He sat by his tenk and ate a sandwich. An ankt was crawling on it. Yuck! Then he saw an ant on his hamd. He was sitting on a whole ness of ants! It made him jum! He fell and broke his arm. Now he has a casp.

WRITE the circled words correctly.

1. _____

2. _____

3. _____

4. _____

5. _____

6. _____

7. _____

Knock Out

CROSS OUT the pictures whose words **don't** end with two consonant sounds together.

WRITE the words for the pictures you didn't cross out.

_____   _____

_____   _____

Spell Food

Word Scramble

UNSCRAMBLE each word and write it correctly. LOOK at the word box for help. CROSS OUT each word in the word box as you make it.

| apple | bread | banana | carrot | cookie | milk | pizza | steak |

SPELLING LIST

apple
banana
bread
carrot
cookie
milk
pizza
steak

1. zapiz   _____

2. kiml   _____

3. racort   _____

4. nnaaab   _____

5. dearb   _____

6. ioeock   _____

7. sekat   _____

8. pleap   _____

Word Hunt

CIRCLE the words from the word box in the grid. Words go down and across, not diagonally or backward.

| apple | bread | banana | carrot | cookie | milk | pizza | steak |

```
b  r  e  a  d  a  n  s
i  b  c  a  r  r  o  t
z  a  o  p  p  a  z  e
z  n  o  p  i  z  z  a
a  a  k  l  m  i  l  k
b  n  i  e  p  p  i  d
b  a  e  i  l  k  p  p
```

WRITE each word that you circled.

_____   _____

_____   _____

_____   _____

Sort and Spell

LISTEN for two consonant sounds together at either the **start** or the **end** of each word pictured. DRAW a line from the picture to the correct sound box. WRITE the word in the box.

<table>
<tr><td>

Start

_____

_____

_____

</td><td>

End

_____

_____

_____

</td></tr>
</table>

Circle It

CIRCLE the pictures with words that have a long vowel sound.

WRITE the words that have
a long vowel sound.

WRITE the words that have
a short vowel sound.

_____

_____

_____

_____

_____

_____

Criss Cross

READ the clues. FILL IN the boxes with the right word for each clue.

Across

1. Covers up a broken arm
3. Hop into the air
6. Male ruler of a country
7. Where birds lay eggs
9. A piece of meat you eat for dinner
11. Red juicy fruit
13. I'm going on a _____ to another state.
15. Yellow fruit with thick skin

Down

1. Sweet, round snack
2. Firefighters drive a fire _____.
4. A belt helps you hold these up
5. The outside part of a sandwich
8. Careful you don't _____ on the wet stairs.
10. Where you sleep when you're camping
12. Round crusty food covered with cheese
14. Help me out. Give me a _____.

Vowels with "R"

Puzzle Pairs

ADD an "r" to the vowel in each word pair to finish the sentence.

SPELLING LIST

card
chart
hard
part
her
chirp
first
skirt
bird
worm
hurt
turn

1. Don't **pat** Carlos on the head. It will mess up the _____ in his hair.

2. That baby bird is a **chip** off the old block. He can _____ like a champ.

3. In the **skit**, Jayla had to wear an ugly _____.

4. I bumped my head going into the **hut**. Boy, did it _____!

5. How do you punch? Making a **fist** is the _____ step.

6. Brit **bid** on an old painting with a _____ in a nest.

7. Dion had a **chat** with the mapmaker, who showed him his best _____.

Herd a Word

WRITE each word from the Spelling List next to the word with the same vowel sound.

girl _____

_____

_____

_____

_____

_____

_____

car _____

_____

_____

_____

Word Scramble

UNSCRAMBLE the words. LOOK at the word box for help. CROSS OUT each word in the word box as you make it.

card	hard	chart	part	her	first	chirp	bird	skirt	worm	hurt	turn

1. drac _____

2. rathc _____

3. adhr _____

4. ridb _____

5. romw _____

6. trifs _____

7. urnt _____

8. thru _____

9. kitrs _____

10. aprt _____

11. criph _____

12. rhe _____

Not Quite!

CIRCLE the words that are misspelled in this story.

It's not hord to play musical chairs. Ferst, you walk around while the music plays. When the music stops, grab a seat! If someone beats you to the seat, let heer have it. Be a good sport. That's port of the game. And don't feel hert. You'll get another torn. It's just like with a berd. The early one gets the werm.

WRITE the circled words correctly.

1. _____   5. _____

2. _____   6. _____

3. _____   7. _____

4. _____   8. _____

Word Split

DRAW lines to connect word beginnings with the correct endings.

SPELLING LIST

more
store
deer
cheer
steer
dear
gear
near
care
dare
share
chair
hair
pair

1.  d  ore

2.  st  air

3.  g  ear

4.  ch  eer

Which Is Which?

FILL IN the missing letters in this e-mail.

D__ __r Mom,

I saw three d__ __r in the yard today.

—Levon

Blank Out

FILL IN the missing "ee" or "ea" in these sentences.

1. Peggy had too much g__ __r when she went camping.

2. I gave her some ice cream to ch__ __r her up

3. It's hard to st__ __r in this driving game.

4. Martha's grandmother was very d__ __r to her.

5. Don't go too n__ __r that barking dog.

Blank Out

FILL IN the missing "air," "are," or "ore" in each word.

1. Thad must learn to

   sh__ __ __ his food.

2. Do you **c**__ __ __ if I skip the game?

3. Zach went to the **st**__ __ __ to buy milk.

4. I got a new **p**__ __ __ of shoes today.

5. Kate climbed the tree on a **d**__ __ __.

6. Please stay in your **ch**__ __ __ during dinner.

7. Oliver asked for **m**__ __ __ food.

8. Tanya likes to admire her **h**__ __ __.

Word Scramble

UNSCRAMBLE each word and write it correctly. LOOK at the word box for help. CROSS OUT each word in the word box as you make it.

more	store	cheer	steer	gear	near	dare	share	chair	pair

1. apir _____

2. ehrec _____

3. reag _____

4. eanr _____

5. hraic _____

6. tesre _____

7. remo _____

8. eard _____

9. hreas _____

10. orste _____

What's the Weather?

Word Hunt

CIRCLE the words from the Spelling List in the grid. Words go across and down, not diagonally or backward.

SPELLING LIST

- cloud
- cold
- rain
- shower
- snow
- warm
- weather
- wind

w	e	a	t	c	w	e	r
a	o	u	d	r	a	i	n
r	a	w	e	i	r	s	c
s	h	o	c	n	m	h	l
n	c	l	o	u	d	o	o
o	n	d	l	i	n	w	u
w	i	n	d	d	w	e	r
w	e	a	t	h	e	r	m

WRITE each word that you circled.

_____   _____

_____   _____

_____   _____

_____

Word Scramble

UNSCRAMBLE each word and write it correctly. LOOK at the Spelling List for help.

1. ianr   _____

2. wamr   _____

3. ocdl   _____

4. dniw   _____

5. rwheeat   _____

6. ludco   _____

7. shwoer   _____

8. nswo   _____

Circle It

LISTEN for the words with the same vowel sound. WRITE the word in the correct box.

HINT: One sound can be spelled different ways.

Sounds like *far*	Sounds like *fur*

Word Scramble

UNSCRAMBLE each word and write it correctly. LOOK at the word box for help. Then CIRCLE all the words that have the same vowel sound as *fur*.

| hard | chart | first | chirp | her | hurt | turn | warm | cold | skirt |

1. hicrp _____

2. rwam _____

3. ruht _____

4. iksrt _____

5. tcrah _____

6. rhe _____

7. tsrfi _____

8. ardh _____

9. dloc _____

10. nrtu _____

Criss Cross

READ the clues. FILL IN the boxes with the right word for each clue.

Across

1. White and puffy in the sky
3. The sun shone and made it _____.
4. To turn the wheel of a car
6. Something to sit on
9. A sudden burst of rain
10. Cold and white, falling from the sky
11. To change your direction
15. Water falling from the sky
16. An animal who lives in the woods

Down

2. A word at the beginning of a letter
3. You choose your outfit based on the _____ outside that day.
4. To give some to someone else
5. Before anything else.
7. She liked to brush _____ hair.
8. When I finish this bowl, I would like some _____.
12. Close by
13. It helps make kites fly when it blows.
14. You switch to a new _____ on your bike when you go uphill.

The Long "A" Way

Sort and Spell

LISTEN for the long **a** sound in each word pictured. DRAW a line from the picture to the box that shows how long **a** is spelled. WRITE the word correctly in the box.

SPELLING LIST

gray
play
say
tray
braid
mail
paint
snail
train
weigh
weight
neighbor

| gray | paint | play | snail | train | tray |

ay	ai

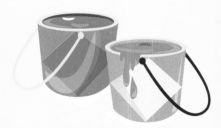

Knock Out

CROSS OUT the pictures that show words **without** the long **a** sound.

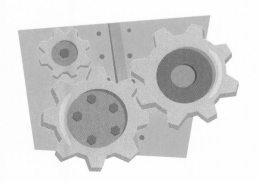

WRITE the words for the pictures you didn't cross out.

_____   _____

_____   _____

The Long "A" Way

Blank Out

FILL IN the missing words in these sentences. LOOK at the word box for help.

say	play	gray	train	mail	paint	weigh	neighbor

1. Shen checked the _____ every day for a letter from his friend.

2. I get on the scale to see how much I _____.

3. Stella's dad takes the _____ to work.

4. Penn wants to _____ his room blue so it feels like the ocean.

5. Sometimes I don't know what to _____ when I meet someone new.

6. Janice likes to _____ on the monkey bars.

7. Tad went next door to meet the new _____.

8. The elephant has tough, _____ skin.

Not Quite!

CIRCLE the words that are misspelled in this story.

I went out to plai. My nayber was checking her mayl. She's kind of old, with gra hair—a lot of hair! She has the biggest brade I ever saw. It must wey a ton. She said, "If I roll up this braid, my head will look like a giant snale!" What do you sae to that?

WRITE the circled words correctly.

1. _____

2. _____

3. _____

4. _____

5. _____

6. _____

7. _____

8. _____

Free with Long "E"

Sort and Spell

LISTEN for the long **e** sound in each word pictured. DRAW a line from the picture to the box that shows how long **e** is spelled. WRITE the word in the box.

SPELLING LIST

green
teeth
tree
wheel
beach
leaf
seal
speak
key
monkey
candy
puppy

beach   green   leaf   seal   teeth   wheel

ea	ee

Riddle Me This!

UNSCRAMBLE the words in the riddles. LOOK at the Spelling List for help.

1. **Q.** What did the dentist say when the **acnyd**-loving **pppyu** showed him her **eteth**?

   _____ _____

   _____

   A. Your bite is worse than your bark.

2. **Q.** A **nmeyok** saw a Spanish sparrow and a French hen in a **rete**. What language did he **eapks**?

   _____ _____

   _____

   A. None. Monkeys can't talk.

Knock Out

CROSS OUT the pictures whose words **don't** have a long **e** sound.

WRITE the words for the pictures you didn't cross out.

_____   _____

_____   _____

Word Scramble

UNSCRAMBLE each word and write it correctly. LOOK at the word box for help.
CROSS OUT each word in the word box as you make it.

green   teeth   wheel   beach   leaf   seal   speak   key   monkey   puppy

1. eelhw _____

2. abche _____

3. slae _____

4. tthee _____

5. mekoyn _____

6. ngree _____

7. kye _____

8. pupyp _____

9. elfa _____

10. ksepa _____

Try Long "I"

Blank Out

FILL IN the missing "i," "igh," or "y" in these sentences.

SPELLING LIST

blind

find

kind

mind

fly

spy

try

bright

high

light

right

sigh

1. What **k___nd** of sandwich do you want?

2. Joel was singing "Three **bl___nd** mice."

3. I know I hate eggplant, so I don't need to **tr___** it.

4. Sierra's bad mood made her mother **s_____**.

5. The cookies are too **h_____** up for me to reach.

6. Taye hid so well they couldn't **f___nd** him.

7. Jay was so **l_____t** I could lift him easily.

8. The sun is too **br_____t** for me to keep sleeping.

Riddle Me This!

UNSCRAMBLE the words in the riddles. LOOK at the Spelling List for help.

1. **Q.** What do you call a desk lamp that gets straight As?

   A. A **bhgitr htigl**.

   _____ _____

2. **Q.** Why did the crazy guy keep turning left?

   A. He wasn't in his **girth nimd**.

   _____ _____

3. **Q.** What has six legs, wings, and buzzes in code?

   A. A **lfy yps**.

   _____ _____

Try Long "I"

Word Hunt

CIRCLE the words from the word box in the grid. Words go down and across, not diagonally or backward.

blind	bright	fly	high	kind	light	mind	try

```
s  f  l  y  i  t  e
b  r  i  g  h  t  n
h  i  g  i  n  r  d
i  f  h  y  k  y  g
g  t  t  g  i  h  s
h  b  l  i  n  d  p
s  m  i  n  d  i  o
```

WRITE each word that you circled.

_____   _____

_____   _____

_____   _____

_____   _____

Word Scramble

UNSCRAMBLE each word and write it correctly. LOOK at the word box for help.
CROSS OUT each word in the word box as you make it.

blind	find	kind	mind	spy	bright	high	light	right	sigh

1. dkin _____

2. fidn _____

3. mnid _____

4. ihhg _____

5. inbdl _____

6. rthibg _____

7. pys _____

8. igrht _____

9. ithlg _____

10. gshi _____

The Long "O" Show

Sort and Spell

LISTEN for the long **o** sound in each word pictured. DRAW a line from the picture to the correct sound box. WRITE the word in the box.

SPELLING LIST

bow
bowl
crow
own
show
slow
boat
coach
goal
goat
road
soap

coach   bow   goat   crow   boat   bowl

oa	ow

Blank Out

FILL IN the missing "oa" or "ow" in these sentences.

1. Let me **sh__ __** you how to do that.

2. Greg was going too **sl__ __**, so I gave him a push.

3. Ayla poured cereal into her **b__ __l**.

4. TJ scored the winning **g__ __l** at the soccer game.

5. Mike doesn't **__ __n** any fancy clothes.

6. The **c__ __ch** showed me a better way to kick the ball.

7. I hold my father's hand when I cross the **r__ __d**.

8. I couldn't find any **s__ __p** for my bath.

Knock Out

CROSS OUT the pictures that show words that **don't** have a long **o** sound.

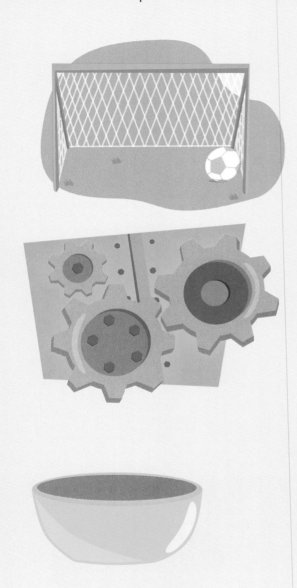

WRITE the words for the pictures you didn't cross out.

_____   _____

_____   _____

Word Scramble

UNSCRAMBLE each word and write it correctly. LOOK at the word box for help.
CROSS OUT each word in the word box as you make it.

bow   crow   own   show   slow   boat   coach   goal   goat   road

1. atob _____

2. rdoa _____

3. wob _____

4. wrco _____

5. algo _____

6. accoh _____

7. onw _____

8. oatg _____

9. oslw _____

10. swho _____

The New, True Long "U"

Blank Out

FILL IN the missing "ue," "ui," "oo," or "ew" in these sentences.

SPELLING LIST

blue
glue
true
fruit
few
flew
chew
threw
boot
broom
moon
tooth

1. Grab a **br____m** and sweep up.

2. I still have a **f____** things to do before we go.

3. Mom always tells me to **ch____** my food before I swallow.

4. None of the things Billy told me about Mars were **tr____**.

5. Tony **thr____** the ball to Jamal.

6. I like to have **fr____t** in my cereal.

7. The sun shone down on the **bl____** sea.

8. Andrea plans to be the first woman on the **m____n**.

Knock Out

CROSS OUT the pictures that show words that **don't** have a long **u** sound.

WRITE the words for the pictures you didn't cross out.

_____   _____

_____   _____

Word Blocks

FILL IN the word blocks with words of the same shape from the word box. Use the pictures as clues.

blue   glue   boot   broom   tooth   fruit

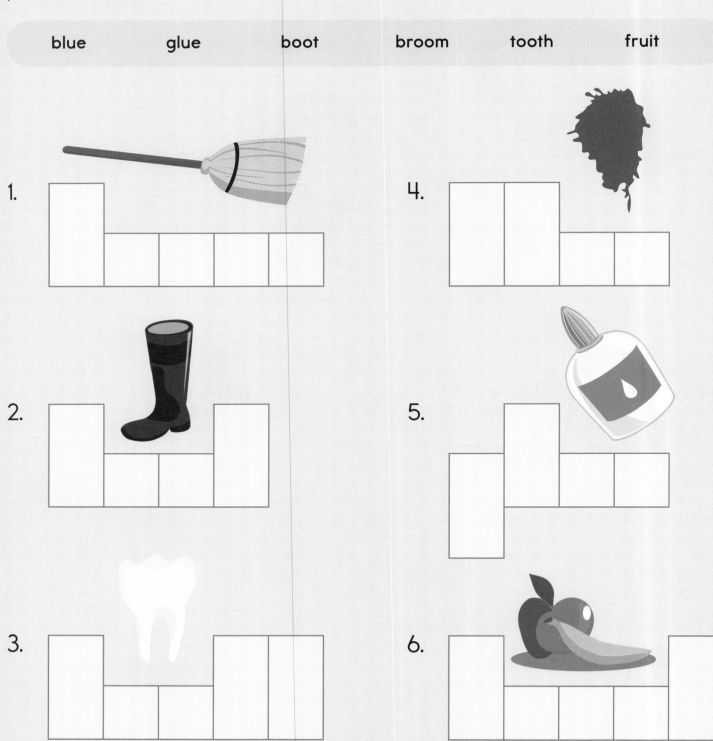

1.

2.

3.

4.

5.

6.

Word Scramble

UNSCRAMBLE each word and write it correctly. LOOK at the word box for help.
CROSS OUT each word in the word box as you make it.

| glue | true | few | chew | threw | flew | boot | broom | moon | tooth |

1. rewht _____

2. efw _____

3. hcwe _____

4. welf _____

5. noom _____

6. rteu _____

7. elgu _____

8. ottho _____

9. rmboo _____

10. oobt _____

Sort and Spell

LISTEN for the long **a** sound or the long **e** sound in each word pictured. DRAW a line from the picture to the correct sound box. WRITE the word in the box.

Long **a**	Long **e**
_____	_____
_____	_____
_____	_____

Circle It

CIRCLE the pictures that show words that have a long **o** sound.

WRITE the words that have a long **o** sound.

_____

_____

_____

_____

The words you didn't circle have what vowel sound?

_____

WRITE those words.

_____

_____

Criss Cross

READ the clues. FILL IN the boxes with the right word for each clue.

Across

1. Do this again if you don't succeed the first time.
2. A young dog
4. The person who lives next door
6. _____ me what's in your hand
8. A very heavy thing
11. What you bring to the post office
12. Bigger and thicker than a shoe
14. An animal that hangs from its tail

Down

1. Your mouth is filled with them
2. To color your walls
3. What gets rid of darkness
5. When it's very light, it's _____.
7. Your bicycle has one in front and one in back.
9. Sweet and yummy treat
10. _____ what's on your mind.
13. To have something for yourself

You Old Soft "C"!

Sort and Spell

The letter "c" can make a hard **k** sound, as in *cook*, or soft **s** sound, as in *twice*. LISTEN for the soft or hard **c** in each word pictured. DRAW a line from the picture to the correct sound box. WRITE the word in the box.

SPELLING LIST

face
race
place
space
trace
ice
mice
nice
price
slice
twice
city
cake
clock

Soft **c**	Hard **c**

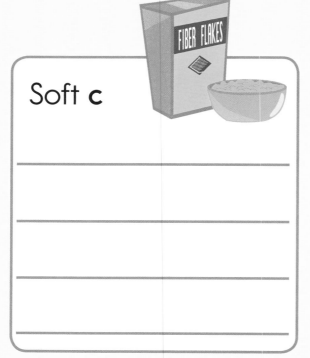

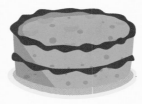
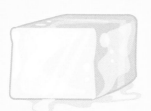

Blank Out

FILL IN the missing "ace" or "ice" to complete words with the soft **c** sound.

1. One way to learn how to draw is to **tr**_____ other pictures.

2. Wipe that smile off your **f**_____, Mister!

3. It was Cale's party, so he had a second **sl**_____ of cake.

4. It was very **n**_____ of you to give me your seat.

5. Someday Bess is going to fly a rocket into **sp**_____.

6. I won't buy this. The **pr**_____ is too high.

7. Fido couldn't find a good **pl**_____ to bury his bone.

8. The cheese goes so fast in our house, Mom says we must have **m**_____.

9. I'll **r**_____ you home!

10. That movie was so good, we watched it **tw**_____.

Match Up

The letter "g" can make both a hard **g** sound, as in *gum,* or a soft **j** sound, as in *age.* WRITE the word from the word box that matches each picture. CIRCLE the pictures that show words that make the **j** sound.

SPELLING LIST

cage

charge

gem

giant

huge

large

page

stage

girl

goat

leg

cage   gem   stage   girl   leg   goat

1

2

3

4

5

6

Word Scramble

UNSCRAMBLE each word and write it correctly. LOOK at the word box for help.
CROSS OUT each word in the word box as you make it.

| cage | charge | gem | giant | huge | large | page | stage |

1. meg   _____

2. aglre   _____

3. ghue   _____

4. hregac   _____

5. gesat   _____

6. intga   _____

7. geap   _____

8. geca   _____

UNSCRAMBLE the words to complete the riddle.

Q. Why did the monster buy a **igtan** battery?

_____

A. He needed a **lrgae hgaerc**.

_____ _____

Spell Special Words

Blank Out

FILL IN the missing word to complete the sentence.

SPELLING LIST

could
might
should
would

1. I **sh**_____ keep looking at these words if I want to learn them.

2. Kayla said she **w**_____ try the spinach.

3. **W**_____ you keep an eye on Scamp?

4. I **m**_____ make it home if the bus ever comes.

5. Jamal **c**_____ do even the hardest math.

6. You **sh**_____ never be afraid to ask.

7. I **c**_____ sure use a hot fudge sundae right now.

Word Hunt

CIRCLE the words from the word box in the grid. Words go across and down, not diagonally or backward. Each word appears twice!

might	could	should	would

```
s  h  o  u  l  d  i  o
r  i  c  o  u  l  d  u
m  w  u  d  c  s  h  l
i  o  m  i  g  h  t  d
g  u  o  u  c  o  u  l
h  l  l  c  o  u  l  d
t  d  w  o  u  l  d  a
l  i  g  h  t  d  o  u
```

WRITE each word that you circled.

_____   _____

_____   _____

Sort and Spell

LISTEN for the soft **c** or soft **g** sound in each word pictured. DRAW a line from the picture to the correct sound box. WRITE the word in the box.

city	face	giant	gem	mice	stage

Soft **c**	Soft **g**
_____	_____
_____	_____
_____	_____

Word Scramble

UNSCRAMBLE each word and write it correctly. LOOK at the word box for help.
CROSS OUT each word in the word box as you make it.

charge giant	place price	stage twice	could should	would might

1. wietc _____

2. angti _____

3. hgcrea _____

4. ulwdo _____

5. ceapl _____

6. getsa _____

7. ldouhs _____

8. rpiec _____

9. hgtmi _____

10. lcodu _____

Criss Cross

FILL IN the grid by answering the clues.

Across

1. He _____ come if he has time.
4. Don't forget to _____ your cell phone so the battery doesn't die.
5. Where you perform a play
6. Two times
8. Small, medium, _____
10. Serving size of cake
13. Was able to
14. A great, big, _____ whale

Down

1. More than one mouse
2. Very big person
3. Rockets go to outer _____.
5. You _____ say "please" when you ask for something.
7. _____ you like some popcorn?
9. To run to see who's fastest
11. Place to keep wild animals
12. This looks like a good _____ to eat.

The Edge of "J"

Blank Out

FILL IN the missing "j" or "dge" to complete the sentence.

SPELLING LIST

bridge
dodge
edge
fudge
hedge
judge
lodge
ridge
jelly
juice
joke

1. Maya loves to eat _____**elly** beans.

2. Deshi is really good at **do**_____ ball.

3. I think a troll lives under this **bri**_____.

4. Lin has a glass of _____**uice** every morning.

5. The scouts had a meeting at the **lo**_____.

6. Mom makes the best **fu**_____ in the world!

7. Max really knows how to tell a _____**oke**.

8. I get scared when I stand too close to the **e**_____.

Write and Rhyme

FILL IN the word from the Spelling List that best fits the picture. Then WRITE another word from the list that rhymes with it.

1

_____

_____

2

_____

_____

3

_____

_____

4

_____

_____

Word Scramble

UNSCRAMBLE each word and write it correctly. Look at the Spelling List for help.

SPELLING LIST

curve
serve
swerve
have
move
prove
dove
glove
love
shove
give
live

1. vepro _____

2. emvo _____

3. lvoeg _____

4. vlei _____

5. ovseh _____

6. aevh _____

7. elov _____

8. eivg _____

9. rseve _____

10. odev _____

11. wreves _____

12. cruve _____

Blank Out!

FILL IN the word from the Spelling List that best fits the sentence.

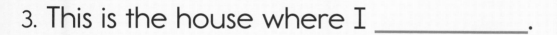

1. Tasha has a mean _____ at Ping-Pong!

2. Please don't _____! We'll all make it onto the bus.

3. This is the house where I _____.

4. During the quake, Dan could feel the earth _____.

5. The car had to _____ so it wouldn't hit the deer.

6. Would you _____ me a hand with this?

7. The sign warned us of a _____ in the road.

8. I think I'll _____ a triple-fudge sundae for dessert.

9. _____, _____, and _____ all rhyme with shove, and I can _____ it!

Silent as a Lamb

Who's Hiding?

LOOK at the word box. CIRCLE the silent letter or letters in each word.
WRITE each word in the box labeled with the silent letter.

| caught | daughter | thumb | knife | lamb | walk |
| talk | knee | wrong | comb | sign | write |

SPELLING LIST

caught
daughter
thumb
comb
lamb
walk
talk
knee
knife
wrong
write
sign

b

g

k

l

w

Not Quite!

CIRCLE the words that are misspelled in this story.

The king said to his dotter, "Your hair is a mess. You need to cowm it."

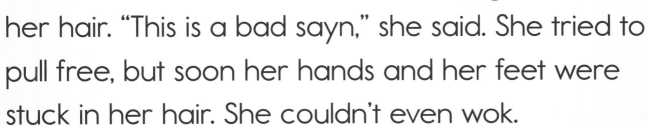

"Rong!" she said. "Tock to the hand!" But she cot her thum in her hair. "This is a bad sayn," she said. She tried to pull free, but soon her hands and her feet were stuck in her hair. She couldn't even wok.

"That's it," said the king. He got a nife and cut her hair short. Now she doesn't need a comb!

WRITE the circled words correctly.

_____   _____

_____   _____

_____   _____

Commonly Misspelled Words

There Their!

There is about a place, and *their* is about people. For example, *Their key was there.* WRITE the right form of *there* or *their* to complete each sentence.

SPELLING LIST

again

because

favorite

friend

people

said

they

there

their

were

_____ were once three little pigs. _____ mother sent them out into the world.
1   2

"Hold on!" said one pig. "_____ are wolves out here!" So they put _____ heads together, and decided to get a house.
                              3   4

"_____ is a nice house," said one pig, pointing to a straw house. "You're kidding, right?" said the others. That was _____ first fight. In the middle of _____ argument, a wolf came by. "_____ is nothing like brick to keep wolves out," he said. He sold them a nice brick house.
     5   6   7   8

"Wait," said the pigs. "Why didn't you eat us?"

"_____ is more money in real estate," said the wolf. He bought a nice steak dinner.
     9

Word Hunt

CIRCLE the words from the word box in the grid. Words go across and down, not diagonally or backward.

| because | they | people | favorite | friend | were | said | again |

```
t  b  r  a  g  a  i  n
h  e  n  d  a  f  r  t
e  c  a  w  e  r  e  h
f  a  v  o  r  i  t  e
s  u  d  r  a  e  p  y
a  s  a  i  n  n  d  a
i  e  o  p  l  d  g  h
d  a  p  e  o  p  l  e
```

WRITE each word that you circled.

_____   _____

_____   _____

_____   _____

_____   _____

Commonly Misspelled Words

Blank Out

WRITE the word from the word box that best fits the sentence.

| because | they | people | favorite | friend | were | said | again |

1. Carlos likes to skate with his _____ Kiki.

2. Some _____ are born lucky.

3. My stomach hurt _____ I ate too much.

4. I didn't hear you. Could you tell me that

    _____?

5. Eddie and Ming bought everything _____

    saw.

6. Jake's mother _____ he was late.

7. _____ you able to

    answer that last question?

8. No one believes that snails

    are my _____ food.

Word Scramble

UNSCRAMBLE each word and write it correctly. LOOK at the word box for help.
CROSS OUT each word in the word box as you make it.

| because | they | people | favorite | their |
| there | friend | were | said | again |

1. aagni _____

2. htire _____

3. iafeotrv _____

4. aesebcu _____

5. nriefd _____

6. erew _____

7. aisd _____

8. eleopp _____

9. yeth _____

10. rheet _____

Circle It

CIRCLE the pictures that show words that have silent letters.

WRITE the words that have a long vowel sound.

_____   _____

_____

Sort and Spell

DRAW a line from the picture to the box that shows the correct word ending. WRITE the word in the box.

bridge	dove	glove	hedge	judge	love

-ve	-dge
_____	_____
_____	_____
_____	_____

Criss Cross

READ the clues. FILL IN the boxes with the right word for each clue.

Across

4. Where the page ends
5. To present something to someone
6. A metal tool you use to cut things
8. Chocolate treat
10. The answer to "why?"
12. Get out of the way
13. He is standing over _____.
14. A bend in the road

Down

1. Where the name of a store is written
2. One more time
3. More than one person
7. The one I like best
8. A person you like
9. A son's sister
10. A way to get across a river
11. I wish you _____ here.

"-Ed" Added

Double or Nothing!

To make a verb past tense, you usually add "-ed." When the verb has a short vowel and ends with one consonant, you usually double the consonant first. WRITE the past tense of each verb in the correct box.

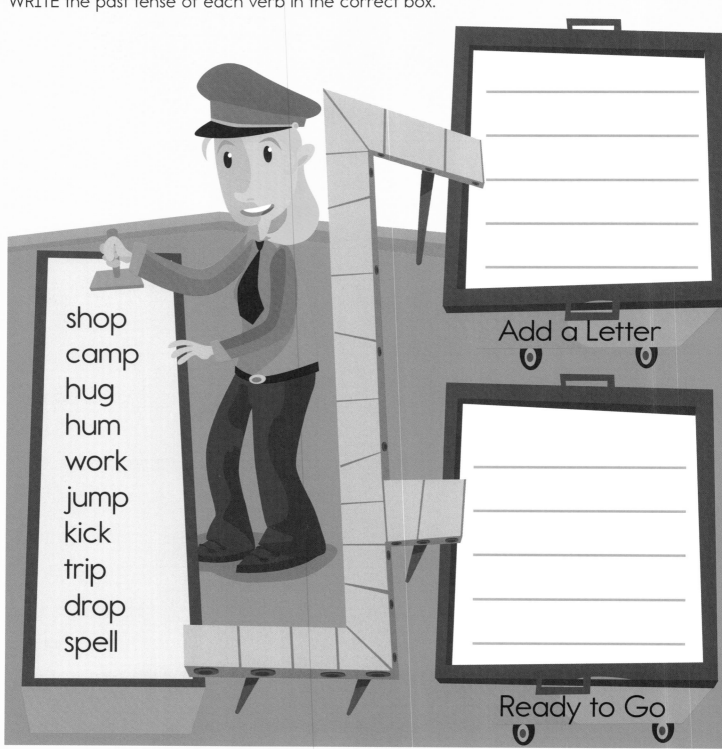

shop
camp
hug
hum
work
jump
kick
trip
drop
spell

Add a Letter

Ready to Go

Make Room!

Usually when a verb ends in "e," you remove the final "e" before adding "ed" to the word. WRITE the past tense of each verb in the correct box.

poke
mark
look
dine
learn
bake
rake
joke
chew
glow

Remove the **e**

Ready to Go

"-Ed" Added

Sort and Spell

READ each word and listen to how it sounds. In some words, the "d" at the end makes a **d** sound. In others, it makes a **t** sound.

MARK each word with a T or a D. Then WRITE the word in the correct word box.

○ hugged

○ seemed

○ kicked

○ tripped

○ served

○ climbed

○ baked

○ jumped

○ piled

○ camped

d
_____
_____
_____
_____
_____

t
_____
_____
_____
_____
_____

Extra Baggage

CIRCLE the words in which the "-ed" adds an extra syllable to the word.
WRITE the words in the correct boxes.

joked

shouted

marked

grinned

tasted

chewed

sipped

darted

rested

nodded

No Extra Baggage

_____

_____

_____

_____

_____

Extra Baggage

_____

_____

_____

_____

_____

The "-Ing" Thing

Samurai Speller!

CROSS OUT the final "e" in the words below.
WRITE the correct form of the word with
"-ing" at the end.

dive + ing = diving

1. bake + ing = _____

2. pile + ing = _____

3. joke + ing = _____

4. serve + ing = _____

5. live + ing = _____

6. poke + ing = _____

7. dine + ing = _____

8. taste + ing = _____

9. prove + ing = _____

10. rake + ing = _____

Double Up

ADD a second consonant to the end of each word. WRITE the correct form of the word with "-ing" on the end.

nod + d + ing = nodding

1. rub   + ____ + ing = _____

2. dip   + ____ + ing = _____

3. drop + ____ + ing = _____

4. plan + ____ + ing = _____

5. hum   + ____ + ing = _____

6. shop + ____ + ing = _____

7. trip + ____ + ing = _____

8. grin + ____ + ing = _____

9. plan + ____ + ing = _____

10. chat + ____ + ing = _____

The "-Ing" Thing

This Way Please!

WRITE the "-ing" form of each word in the correct box. CROSS OUT each word as you write it.

taste

shop

dive

hug

mark

serve

camp

lock

drop

bake

joke

sip

plan

gulp

kick

Double Final Consonant

_____

_____

_____

_____

_____

Drop Final **e**

_____

_____

_____

_____

_____

Leave Alone

_____

_____

_____

_____

Two's Company

WRITE the plural form of each word by adding "-s" to the end.

1. pig   + ____ = _____

2. cape   + ____ = _____

3. path   + ____ = _____

4. belt   + ____ = _____

5. stick   + ____ = _____

6. truck   + ____ = _____

7. king   + ____ = _____

8. lamp   + ____ = _____

9. nest   + ____ = _____

10. carrot   + ____ = _____

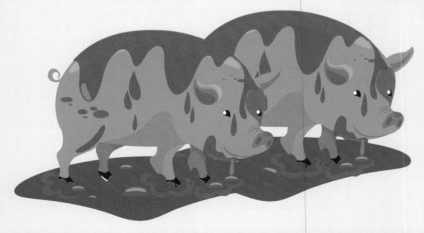

To "E" or Not to "E"

ADD an "-es" to these words to make them plural.

1. glass + _____ = _____

2. witch + _____ = _____

3. dish + _____ = _____

4. fox + _____ = _____

5. lash + _____ = _____

6. wish + _____ = _____

7. guess + _____ = _____

8. bus + _____ = _____

9. miss + _____ = _____

10. box + _____ = _____

11. watch + _____ = _____

12. itch + _____ = _____

Sort and Spell

LISTEN for the sound the "s" makes at the end of each word. DRAW a line from the picture to the correct sound box. WRITE the word in the box.

bananas	books	chairs	girls	sticks	trucks

s

_____

_____

_____

z

_____

_____

_____

Extra Baggage

CIRCLE the words where the "s" or "es" adds an extra syllable to the word.
WRITE the words in the correct boxes.

glasses

showers

witches

itches

boots

carrots

cards

buses

baths

matches

No Extra Baggage

_____

_____

_____

_____

_____

Extra Baggage

_____

_____

_____

_____

_____

Word Scramble

Some words form plurals in unusual ways:

End in EN	OO → EE	OUSE → ICE	No Change
man → men woman → women child → children	foot → feet tooth → teeth	mouse → mice	sheep deer fish

UNSCRAMBLE each word and write it correctly. LOOK at the word box for help.

1. ftee _____

2. meonw _____

3. tehet _____

4. cmie _____

5. delicrnh _____

Word Hunt

CIRCLE the plural words from the word box in the grid. Words go across and down, not diagonally or backward.

men   women   children   feet   teeth   mice   deer   sheep   fish

```
f  i  m  w  o  m  e  n
m  o  u  n  e  g  t  w
i  c  f  e  e  t  e  o
c  h  i  l  d  r  e  n
e  o  s  f  e  w  t  d
e  s  h  e  e  p  h  r
m  e  n  e  r  e  n  e
```

WRITE each word that you circled.

_____   _____

_____   _____

_____   _____

_____   _____

"-Er" and "-Est"

Blank Out

FILL IN the missing "-er" or "-est" in these sentences.

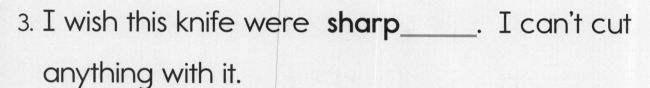

1. Chip is pretty tall, but Jason is

   tall_____.

2. King Midas must have been the

   rich_____ person in the world!

3. I wish this knife were **sharp_____**. I can't cut

   anything with it.

4. This is the **soft_____** pillow I've ever had.

5. Mom was proud of me for winning the game, but

   even **proud_____** for being a good sport.

6. If this hill gets any **steep_____**, I won't be able to get

   to the top.

7. Lola thought she had the **kind_____** grandmother

   ever!

So Lonesome...

When a word has a short vowel sound and ends with one consonant, double that consonant before adding "-er" or "-est."

DOUBLE the last consonant. WRITE the correct form of each word.

1. big + _____ + er = _____

2. fat + _____ + est = _____

3. sad + _____ + est = _____

4. dim + _____ + er = _____

5. red + _____ + er = _____

6. fit + _____ + est = _____

7. tan + _____ + est = _____

8. wet + _____ + er = _____

9. hot + _____ + est = _____

10. fat + _____ + er = _____

11. big + _____ + est = _____

12. sad + _____ + er = _____

"-Er" and "-Est"

Samurai Speller!

CROSS OUT the final "e" in the words. WRITE the correct form of the word with "-er" or "-est" at the end.

1. nice + er = _____

2. fine + est = _____

3. safe + er = _____

4. stale + est = _____

5. brave + er = _____

6. white + er = _____

7. wise + est = _____

8. rude + er = _____

9. late + est = _____

10. ripe + est = _____

Not Quite!

CIRCLE the words that are misspelled in this story.

The bigest mistake I made was staying latter than I should have. The sky was getting darkker. The wind was blowing the wilddest I had ever seen. Mom, who's oldder and wisser than I am, said I should hurry home. "I'm not scared," I said. "I'm braveer than that."

Brave, maybe, but not the smarttest.

It rained hardder than ever. When I got home, I was weter than I'd ever been.

WRITE the circled words correctly.

1. _____

2. _____

3. _____

4. _____

5. _____

6. _____

7. _____

8. _____

9. _____

10. _____

Quick Change

CROSS OUT the final "y" in each word and change it to an "i." Then WRITE the correct form of the word with "-er" or "-est."

1. dry   + _____ + er   = _____

2. lovely   + _____ + est   = _____

3. pretty   + _____ + est   = _____

4. skinny   + _____ + er   = _____

5. noisy   + _____ + er   = _____

6. funny   + _____ + est   = _____

7. ugly   + _____ + est   = _____

8. heavy   + _____ + er   = _____

9. lucky   + _____ + est   = _____

10. early   + _____ + er   = _____

11. sandy   + _____ + est   = _____

12. friendly + _____ + er   = _____

Word Hunt

CIRCLE the words from the word box in the grid. Words go across and down, not diagonally or backward.

driest   earlier   funniest   goofiest   heaviest   meatier   prettier   tastier

e	r	o	g	o	o	f	i	e	s	t
a	e	s	t	p	r	e	d	i	e	a
r	o	o	f	y	d	o	r	b	d	s
l	e	a	f	u	n	n	i	e	s	t
i	p	r	e	t	t	i	e	r	s	i
e	h	e	a	v	i	e	s	t	i	e
r	f	u	n	m	e	a	t	i	e	r

WRITE each word that you circled.

_____   _____

_____   _____

_____   _____

_____   _____

Review

This Way Please!

WRITE the "-er" form of each word in the correct box. CROSS OUT each word as you write it.

skinny

dry

wet

heavy

ripe

big

brave

nice

wise

noisy

sad

funny

fine

fat

hot

Double Final Consonant

_____

_____

_____

_____

Drop Final **e**

_____

_____

_____

_____

Change **y** to **i**

_____

_____

_____

_____

Word Scramble

UNSCRAMBLE each word and write it correctly. LOOK at the word box for help.
CROSS OUT each word in the word box as you make it.

bravest	older	loveliest	strangest	smaller	richest
skinniest	clearest	cleaner	bigger	stronger	wiser

1. agrstenst _____

2. bgeigr _____

3. grersnot _____

4. arnlece _____

5. slelrma _____

6. eeilvtlso _____

7. aeseltcr _____

8. elrdo _____

9. sitskneni _____

10. streich _____

11. avsebtr _____

12. sweri _____

Answers

Page 2
1. big bug
2. hot hat
3. bad bed
4. nut net
5. hip hop

Page 3
ACROSS   DOWN
1. cat   2. top
3. mop   4. pup
6. pet   5. hit
8. pit   7. tub
10. tag   9. ten
11. bed

Page 4
1. hope, hop
2. made, mad
3. pet, Pete
4. cute, cut
5. fine, fin

Page 5
1. cut → cute
2. gav → gave
3. pok → poke
4. mad → made
5. hid → hide
6. hat → hate
7. hop → hope
8. tim → time

Page 6
1. white
2. chop
3. thick
4. shop
5. chat
6. ship
7. thin
8. when

Page 7
1. chick
2. white
3. shapes
4. ship
5. chop
6. shop

Page 8
1. ship
2. thin
3. what
4. chick
5. white
6. chop
7. chat
8. shapes
9. thick
10. shop

Page 9
1. thick, thin
2. chick chat
3. ship shape

Page 10
1. fish
2. with
3. which
4. watch
5. dash
6. math
7. witch
8. catch

Page 11
1. bath
2. rich
3. catch
4. dash

Page 12
1. math
2. rich
3. watch
4. bath
5. fish
6. witch

Page 13
1. whish → which
2. wich → witch
3. ritsh → rich
4. catsh → catch
5. fich → fish
6. maf → math
7. wif → with
8. datsh → dash

Page 14
1. dress
2. skirt
3. shirt
4. coat
5. shoe
6. belt
7. shorts
8. pants

Page 15

Page 16
ch: chop, chick, rich
sh: fish, shoe, ship

Page 17
watch, witch, catch

Pages 18–19
ACROSS   DOWN
3. which   1. shape
5. ship   2. shirt
7. thin   4. shorts
8. thick   6. fish
10. chop   9. chick
13. white   11. pants
14. catch   12. belt
15. math   14. chat

Page 20
Cross out: duck, kite
Write: truck, frog, stick, slide

Page 21
1. clam
2. spill
3. trap
4. frog
5. steps
6. crab

Page 22
1. truck
2. frog
3. stick
4. trap
5. slip
6. crab
7. slide
8. trip

Page 23
1. slip
2. trap
3. steps
4. clam
5. stick
6. crab
7. stop
8. spill
9. slide
10. trip
11. frog
12. truck

Pages 24–25
1. hand
2. desk
3. lamp
4. gift
5. nest
6. mask
7. jump
8. tent
9. cast
10. ant
11. camp
12. band

Page 26
1. capm → camp
2. tenk → tent
3. ankt → ant
4. hamd → hand
5. ness → nest
6. jum → jump
7. casp → cast

Page 27
Cross out: fan, clam, key
Write: desk, lamp, gift, mask

Page 28
1. pizza
2. milk
3. carrot
4. banana
5. bread
6. cookie
7. steak
8. apple

Page 29

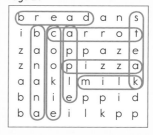

Page 30
Start: trap, slide, frog
End: mask, tent, lamp

Page 31
Long vowel: shapes, white, slide
Short vowel: truck, desk, spill

Pages 32–33
ACROSS   DOWN
1. cast   1. cookie
3. jump   2. truck
6. king   4. pants
7. nest   5. bread
9. steak   8. slip
11. apple   10. tent
13. trip   12. pizza
15. banana   14. hand

Page 34
1. part
2. chirp
3. skirt
4. hurt
5. first
6. bird
7. chart

Page 35
girl: her, chirp, first, hurt, turn, bird, skirt, worm
car: card, chart, hard, part

Page 36
1. card
2. chart
3. hard
4. bird
5. worm
6. first
7. turn
8. hurt
9. skirt
10. part
11. chirp
12. her

Page 37
1. hord → hard
2. ferst → first
3. heer → her
4. port → part
5. hert → hurt
6. torn → turn
7. berd → bird
8. werm → worm

Answers

Page 38
1. deer
2. store
3. gear
4. chair

Page 39
Dear, deer

1. gear
2. cheer
3. steer
4. dear
5. near

Page 40
1. share
2. care
3. store
4. pair
5. dare
6. chair
7. more
8. hair

Page 41
1. pair
2. cheer
3. gear
4. near
5. chair
6. steer
7. more
8. dare
9. share
10. store

Page 42

Page 43
1. rain
2. warm
3. cold
4. wind
5. weather
6. cloud
7. shower
8. snow

Page 44
far: car, cards, yarn
fur: bird, skirt, worm

Page 45
1. chirp
2. warm
3. hurt
4. skirt
5. chart
6. her
7. first
8. hard
9. cold
10. turn

Circle: chirp, hurt, her, first, turn

Pages 46–47
ACROSS DOWN
1. cloud 2. dear
3. warm 3. weather
4. steer 4. share
6. chair 5. first
9. shower 7. her
10. snow 8. more
11. turn 12. near
15. rain 13. wind
16. deer 14. gear

Page 48
ay: gray, play, tray
ai: paint, train, snail

Page 49
Cross out: car, gear
Write: weight, mail, braid, snail

Page 50
1. mail
2. weigh
3. train
4. paint
5. say
6. play
7. neighbor
8. gray

Page 51
1. plai → play
2. nayber → neighbor
3. mayl → mail
4. gra → gray
5. brade → braid
6. wey → weigh
7. snale → snail
8. sae → say

Page 52
ea: beach, leaf, seal
ee: green, teeth, wheel

Page 53
1. candy, puppy, teeth
2. monkey, tree, speak

Page 54
Cross out: worm, yo-yo
Write: key, candy, tree, puppy

Page 55
1. wheel
2. beach
3. seal
4. teeth
5. monkey
6. green
7. key
8. puppy
9. leaf
10. speak

Page 56
1. kind
2. blind
3. try
4. sigh
5. high
6. find
7. light
8. bright

Page 57
1. bright light
2. right mind
3. fly spy

Page 58

Page 59
1. kind
2. find
3. mind
4. high
5. blind
6. bright
7. spy
8. right
9. light
10. sigh

Page 60
oa: boat, coach, goat
ow: bow, bowl, crow

Page 61
1. show
2. slow
3. bowl
4. goal
5. own
6. coach
7. road
8. soap

Page 62
Cross out: gear, fork
Write: goal, soap, road, bowl

Page 63
1. boat
2. road
3. bow
4. crow
5. goal
6. coach
7. own
8. goat
9. slow
10. show

Page 64
1. broom
2. few
3. chew
4. true
5. threw
6. fruit
7. blue
8. moon

Page 65
Cross out: watch, girl
Write: blue, moon, glue, fruit

Page 66
1. broom
2. boot
3. tooth
4. blue
5. glue
6. fruit

Page 67
1. threw
2. few
3. chew
4. flew
5. moon
6. true
7. glue
8. tooth
9. broom
10. boot

Page 68
Long a: braid, mail, weight
Long e: beach, gear, leaf

Page 69
Long o: soap, bowl, coach, boat
Long u: moon, broom

Pages 70–71
ACROSS DOWN
1. try 1. teeth
2. puppy 2. paint
4. neighbor 3. light
6. show 5. bright
8. weight 7. wheel
11. mail 9. candy
12. boot 10. say
14. monkey 13. own

Page 72
Soft c: face, ice, city, mice
Hard c: clock, cake

Page 73
1. trace
2. face
3. slice
4. nice
5. space
6. price
7. place
8. mice
9. race
10. twice

Page 74
1. gem
2. leg
3. cage
4. goat
5. girl
6. stage
Circle: gem, cage, stage

Page 75
1. gem
2. large
3. huge
4. charge
5. stage
6. giant
7. page
8. cage

Riddle: giant, large charge

Page 76
1. should
2. would
3. Would
4. might
5. could
6. should
7. could

Page 77

```
s h o u l d  i  o
r  i  c o u l d  u
m w u d c s h l
i  o  m i g h t  d
g u o u c o u l
h  l  l  c o u l d
t  d w o u l d a
l  i  g h t d o u
```

Page 78
Soft c: mice, face, city
Soft g: giant, gem, stage

Page 79
1. twice
2. giant
3. charge
4. would
5. place
6. stage
7. should
8. price
9. might
10. could

Pages 80–81
ACROSS   DOWN
1. might   1. mice
4. charge   2. giant
5. stage   3. space
6. twice   5. should
8. large   7. would
10. slice   9. race
13. could   11. cage
14. huge   12. place

Page 82
1. jelly
2. dodge
3. bridge
4. juice
5. lodge
6. fudge
7. joke
8. edge

Page 83
1. judge, fudge
2. bridge, ridge
3. lodge, dodge
4. hedge, edge

Page 84
1. prove
2. move
3. glove
4. live
5. shove
6. have
7. love
8. give
9. serve
10. dove
11. swerve
12. curve

Page 85
1. serve
2. shove
3. live
4. move
5. swerve
6. give
7. curve
8. have
9. Dove, glove, love, prove

Page 86
b: comb, thumb, lamb
g: caught, daughter, sign
k: knee, knife
l: walk, talk
w: wrong, write

Page 87
1. dotter → daughter
2. cowm → comb
3. rong → wrong
4. tock → talk
5. cot → caught
6. thum → thumb
7. sayn → sign
8. wok → walk
9. nife → knife

Page 88
1. There
2. Their
3. There
4. their
5. There
6. their
7. their
8. There
9. There

Page 89

```
t  b  r  a g a i n
h  e  n  d a f  r  t
e  c  a w e r e h
f  a  v o r  i  t  e
s  u  d r  a e p y
a  s  a  i  n n d a
i  e  o  p  l  d g h
d  a  p e o p l  e
```

Page 90
1. friend
2. people
3. because
4. again
5. they
6. said
7. Were
8. favorite

Page 91
1. again
2. their
3. favorite
4. because
5. friend
6. were
7. said
8. people
9. they
10. there

Page 92
Circle: thumb, knee, comb, knife
Write: knee, comb, knife

Page 93
-ve: dove, glove, love
-dge: bridge, hedge, judge

Pages 94–95
ACROSS   DOWN
4. edge   1 sign
5. give   2. again
6. knife   3. people
8. fudge   7. favorite
10. because 8. friend
12. dodge   9. daughter
13. there   10. bridge
14. curve   11. were

Page 96
Add a Letter: shopped, hugged, hummed, tripped, dropped
Ready to Go: camped, worked, jumped, kicked, spelled

Page 97
Remove the e: poked, dined, baked, raked, joked
Ready to Go: marked, looked, learned, chewed, glowed

Page 98
d: served, piled, seemed, climbed, hugged
t: kicked, jumped, tripped, camped, baked

Page 99
No extra baggage: joked, chewed, sipped, grinned, marked
Extra baggage (circled): shouted, darted, rested, tasted, nodded

Page 100
1. baking
2. piling
3. joking
4. serving
5. living
6. poking
7. dining
8. tasting
9. proving
10. raking

Page 101
1. b, rubbing
2. p, dipping
3. p, dropping
4. n, planning
5. m, humming
6. p, shopping
7. p, tripping
8. n, grinning
9. n, planning
10. t, chatting

Pages 102–103
Drop Final e: diving, tasting, serving, joking, baking
Double Final Consonant: shopping, hugging, sipping, dropping, planning
Leave Alone: gulping, locking, camping, marking, kicking

Page 104
1. s, pigs
2. s, capes
3. s, paths
4. s, belts
5. s, sticks
6. s, trucks
7. s, kings
8. s, lamps
9. s, nests
10. s, carrots

Answers

Page 105
1. es, glasses
2. es, witches
3. es, dishes
4. es, foxes
5. es, lashes
6. es, wishes
7. es, guesses
8. es, buses
9. es, misses
10. es, boxes
11. es, watches
12. es, itches

Page 106
s: books, sticks, trucks
z: bananas, girls, chairs

Page 107
Extra baggage (circled): glasses, witches, itches, matches, buses
No extra baggage: cards, showers, boots, baths, carrots

Page 108
1. feet
2. women
3. teeth
4. mice
5. children

Page 109

Page 110
1. taller
2. richest
3. sharper
4. softest
5. prouder
6. steeper
7. kindest

Page 111
1. g, bigger
2. t, fattest
3. d, saddest
4. m, dimmer
5. d, redder
6. t, fittest
7. n, tannest
8. t, wetter
9. t, hottest
10. t, fatter
11. g, biggest
12. d, sadder

Page 112
1. nicer
2. finest
3. safer
4. stalest
5. braver
6. whiter
7. wisest
8. ruder
9. latest
10. ripest

Page 113
1. bigest → biggest
2. latter → later
3. darkker → darker
4. wilddest → wildest
5. oldder → older
6. wisser → wiser
7. braveer → braver
8. smarttest → smartest
9. hardder → harder
10. weter → wetter

Page 114
1. i, drier
2. i, loveliest
3. i, prettiest
4. i, skinnier
5. i, noisier
6. i, funniest
7. i, ugliest
8. i, heavier
9. i, luckiest
10. i, earlier
11. i, sandiest
12. i, friendlier

Page 115

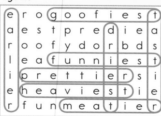

Pages 116–117
Drop Final e: finer, wiser, braver, riper, nicer
Double Final Consonant: fatter, wetter, hotter, sadder, bigger
Change y to i: skinnier, funnier, heavier, drier, noisier

Page 118
1. strangest
2. bigger
3. stronger
4. cleaner
5. smaller
6. loveliest
7. clearest
8. older
9. skinniest
10. richest
11. bravest
12. wiser

Sylvan Workbooks and Learning Kits Help Kids Catch Up, Keep Up, and Get Ahead!

Sylvan is the country's leading provider of supplemental education services in reading, mathematics, and homework support. For more than thirty years and with more than two million success stories, Sylvan has been helping children in grades pre-K–12 realize their potential, whether it's to improve a report card or get ahead for the following school year.

Workbooks use a systematic, age and grade-appropriate approach that helps children find, restore, or strengthen their reading and language-arts skills.

Super Workbooks include three workbooks in one low-priced package!

Also available: 3rd, 4th, and 5th grade workbooks, super workbooks, and learning kits.

All of Sylvan Learning's programs are aligned with their subject-specific industry association, and our products are created in conjunction with Sylvan's highly credentialed educational research and development team.

KINDERGARTEN

Reading Readiness (Workbook)
978-0-375-43020-6 - $12.99/$15.50 Can.

Alphabet Activities (Workbook)
978-0-375-43022-0 - $12.99/$15.50 Can.

Beginning Word Games (Workbook)
978-0-375-43021-3 - $12.99/$15.50 Can.

Language Arts Success (Super Workbook)
978-0-375-43029-9 - $18.99/$22.00 Can.

1ST GRADE

Reading Skill Builders (Workbook)
978-0-375-43023-7 - $12.99/$15.50 Can.

Spelling Games & Activities (Workbook)
978-0-375-43025-1 - $12.99/$15.50 Can.

Vocabulary Puzzles (Workbook)
978-0-375-43024-4 - $12.99/$15.50 Can.

Language Arts Success (Super Workbook)
978-0-375-43030-5 - $18.99/$22.00 Can.

2ND GRADE

Reading Skill Builders (Workbook)
978-0-375-43026-8 - $12.99/$15.50 Can.

Spelling Games & Activities (Workbook)
978-0-375-43028-2 - $12.99/$15.50 Can.

Vocabulary Puzzles (Workbook)
978-0-375-43027-5 - $12.99/$15.50 Can.

Language Arts Success (Super Workbook)
978-0-375-43031-2 - $18.99/$22.00 Can.

All workbooks include a coupon for great savings off your child's Skills Assessment at a Sylvan Learning Center.

Find Sylvan Learning Products at bookstores everywhere and online at:
sylvanlearningbookstore.com

SPECIAL OFFER FROM

Congratulations on your Sylvan product purchase! Your child is now on the way to building skills for further academic success. Sylvan would like to extend a special offer for a discount on our exclusive Sylvan Skills Assessment® to you and your family. Bring this coupon to your scheduled assessment to receive your discount. Limited time offer.* One per family.

You are entitled to a $10 DISCOUNT on a Sylvan Skills Assessment®

This assessment is a comprehensive evaluation of your child's specific strengths and needs using our unique combination of standardized tests, diagnostic tools, and personal interviews. It is an important step in pinpointing the skills your child needs and creating a customized tutoring program just for your child.

Visit www.sylvanlearningproducts.com/coupon today to find a participating location and schedule your Sylvan Skills Assessment®.

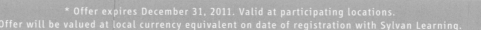